The Colour of Steam

The Colour of Steam — Volume 7

East Coast Main Line—Retford

by **KEITH R. PIRT**

FRONT COVER: Gresley A4 pacific 60033 *Seagull* heads a Newcastle to King's Cross express just south of the Retford GN/GC 'square' crossing in November 1961; semaphore signals, the crossing box and the lovely white steam exhaust make an attractive picture. *Seagull* was the penultimate member of the A4 class, being constructed at Doncaster in June 1938 (Works No 1876) with a Kylchap double chimney from new. It was also one of the first A4s to be withdrawn, in December 1962.

ABOVE: Gresley Class A3 60109 *Hermit*, complete with Kylchap double chimney and German type smoke deflectors, passes Retford North signal box and diverts from the up main to the Platform 1 line with a semi-fast from Leeds Central to King's Cross in November 1961. Gangers at work on the up main line add to the classic scene and *Hermit*

has steam to spare. This engine was an early member of the class, being built in July 1923 at Doncaster (Works No 1570) as an A1 pacific. It was rebuilt in November 1943 to Class A3, fitted with Kylchap double chimney in March 1959 and trough deflectors in January 1961. Withdrawal came in December 1962, its final mileage being 2,076,427.

REAR COVER: Class K1 2-6-0 62054 rounds the curve from the up main line to the Lincoln line at Retford station with an eastbound train of coal wagons on a lovely afternoon in September 1962. The Peppercorn K1 moguls were recent transfers to Retford GC shed replacing the reduced ranks of ex-GC Class J11 and O4 locomotives. A November 1949 built engine (North British Loco Co — Works No 26658), 62054 was withdrawn in December 1964.

Designed by **BARNABUS**
Printed by **Century Litho, Penryn, Cornwall**
Bound by **Booth Bookbinders, Penryn, Cornwall**

ISBN 0-906899-34-6   First published 1989

© TEXT and PHOTOGRAPHS: KEITH R. PIRT

No part of this publication may be reproduced in any form or by any means without the prior written permission of the publishers.

Published by:
ATLANTIC TRANSPORT PUBLISHERS
Waterside House, Falmouth Road,
Penryn, Cornwall TR10 8BE, England.

Introduction

The end of the BR 1962-3 winter timetable in June 1963, whilst not a point in time as infamous as that fateful August day five years later, saw the death knell of scheduled main line steam passenger working on the Great Northern section of the East Coast main line. In just five years full steam express workings from Scotland, the North East, Yorkshire and Lincolnshire to King's Cross had been replaced by new main line diesels and Top Shed (King's Cross) was no more.

From my then home in Sheffield, numerous visits (mainly at weekends but also on holiday weekdays) were made to the line during those last five years of steam. Retford became the focus of attention mainly because of the intersection of the Great Central and Great Northern main lines and the presence of 3½ miles of Gamston bank to Markham Moor summit south of Retford. Along with three other photographers, visits were regular whenever the sun shone; winter or summer made no difference, in fact cold weather was preferred. The booking clerk at Sheffield Victoria came to know us well and had the tickets ready before we arrived at his window. Journeys behind the B1, K3, K2 and D11 classes were numerous in the first two years before the new DMU units inevitably replaced these engines.

At Retford, all classes of main line pacifics, not to mention V2s, K3s etc were seen over the period and it is safe to say that every pacific repaired at Doncaster would have graced Retford's metals at that time. The two Retford sheds, the old Great Northern (GN) near the west side of the station and the former Great Central (GC) just beyond Thrumpton crossing on the south side of the line to Lincoln and Grimsby, initially housed about 45 engines of Classes B1, 02, 04, J6, J11, J39 and N5. Classes K1, WD, and LM Class 4 2-6-0 came there later. All the engines were cleaned, passenger and freight; and the B1 pilot engine in the siding at the North East of

Retford station was a sight to behold. The Gresley Class 02 2-8-0 engines in all their variants were also cleaned and became firm favourites on coal, iron ore and freight workings, lasting to the end of 1963 at Retford GC shed.

Colour photography in 1958 was just beginning to become appreciated by railway photographers and numerous difficulties were met. High quality cameras were subject to import restrictions and were not available in profusion, while transparency film was slow (Kodachrome 1 — 8 ASA); and although 50 ASA film was available, it was grainy and less sharp. Kodachrome 1 was the standard film and initially a Retina IIIC camera with $f2$ Xenon lens was used, although only to a maximum of 1/250 second exposure. This was too slow and at the end of 1959 a Leica M2 camera with f1.4 Summilux lens became standard equipment. The extra lens speed and variable width focal plane shutter gave numerous possible shutter speeds, making it an ideal instrument.

Kodachrome 1 film suffered from reciprocity failure using shutter speeds faster than 1/125 second: at 1/250 it was rated at 6 ASA and became as slow as 4 ASA at 1/500 second. The introduction of 25 ASA Kodachrome II film in August 1961 was the answer: a faster, sharper film without reciprocity failure, thus making it a firm favourite.

The locomotives working on the GN main line were, of course, the real stars and the clean pacifics from Top Shed were our

---

BELOW: Gresley Class V2 2-6-2 60854 heads the morning Edinburgh to King's Cross fast fitted freight past a superb array of semaphore and shunting signals south of Retford crossing in October 1958. The loco is in lined green livery with the first type of BR emblem. In the early days after nationalisation, the V2s were given the lined black mixed traffic livery — perhaps more appropriate to their role. The express passenger green livery replaced this in the 1950s. Also note the single up home signal at the station which had temporarily replaced the up home gantry demolished in an accident.

favourites. Nearly all the A4 class had been rebuilt by mid-1958 with Kylchap double chimneys and the A3 class were being rebuilt; so by the end of 1959 virtually all the East Coast pacifics were Kylchap engines. The exceptions were some Peppercorn A2 class engines which only visited Retford after repair at Doncaster. It is impossible to cover them all in this book although the A4 and A3 classes dominate. All too soon, however, the last A4 with a chalked smokebox door epitaph worked north from King's Cross. Finally, just before the end, Stanier pacific 46245 *City of London* graced the ox-eye daisy-clad Gamston bank on a special train and completed the scene.

My thanks go to the numerous railwaymen who became friends on the trackside, to the PR and PO at Liverpool Street who readily granted lineside photographic facilities but mostly to the steam depots whose locomotives and crews were the real heroes of that time.

Lastly, I am indebted to the RCTS whose volumes of detailed information were invaluable in the compilation of this work.

Keith R Pirt, Chesterfield

BELOW: Peppercorn Class A1 4-6-2 60160 *Auld Reekie* starts a King's Cross to Leeds semi-fast away from Platform 2 at Retford Station North in the final stages of running in from Doncaster shed before returning north to 'Auld Reekie' — Edinburgh. The A1s were the last in a long line of LNER pacifics, the main series emerging in 1948-9. During early BR days, they bore the brunt of the heavier workings on the East Coast main line at a time when the older and well-used Gresley pacifics were under something of a cloud, having suffered much during the 1940s.

A4 Hauled Expresses

ABOVE: Class A4 60014 *Silver Link* has just arrived at Retford Station with the 10.20 am semi-fast from Leeds to King's Cross in June 1962. The normal up gantry can be noted. This engine had just six months to run before withdrawal in December 1962. The second most famous A4, *Silver Link* was the pioneer engine built, in September 1935 with silver and grey livery for the 'Silver Jubilee' express; a Kylchap double chimney was fitted in October 1957. After withdrawal, 60014 was reserved for eight months at Doncaster by Sir Billy Butlin for possible display at his Skegness camp; negotiations broke down when the full restoration to original condition was refused and the engine was scrapped — a sad loss to all Gresley enthusiasts.

BELOW: In this view, 60013 *Dominion of New Zealand* approaches Retford with the down 'Tees-Tyne Pullman' from King's Cross to Newcastle in August 1961. One of five A4s named after major British Colonies and originally designated for use on the 'Coronation' express of 1937, 60013 was, when new, one of the first A4s to carry the Garter Blue livery, later adopted as the standard LNER colour scheme for the whole class. It also carried a whistle donated in May 1939 by the New Zealand Government Railways. A June 1937 built engine, Doncaster Works No 1857, 60013 gained a Kylchap double chminey in July 1958 and was finally withdrawn in June 1963. The NZGR whistle was later acquired by the Ffestiniog Railway.

Fitted Freights

BELOW: BR Standard Class 9F 2-10-0 92149 of New England shed heads an up fitted cement train south of Retford crossing in November 1960. The Class 9Fs were the only really new steam locomotive concept to emerge after Nationalisation and they were arguably the best of all the BR standard types. None of the old companies had anything quite as good or powerful. Sadly, their lives were brought to a premature end by the events of the 1960s. Built at Crewe works to order E494 in October 1957; 92149 was withdrawn in June 1965, less than eight years later, spending nine months in store at Langwith Junction before being cut up by Wards at Beighton, Sheffield.

ABOVE: Class V2 60983, a King's Cross engine, heads the up 'Scotch' fast fitted freight near the River Idle bridge on a lovely morning in November 1960. The use of the word 'Scotch' rather than 'Scottish', though anathema to many Scotsmen, was a very common feature of railway operating between England and Scotland in steam days. No 60983 was the final locomotive of the class to be built (in July 1944 at Darlington — Works No 1936) and although four more were ordered, these were actually built as Class A2/1 4-6-2s with V2 boilers to LNER Engine Diagram 109.

Crossing The River Idle

ABOVE: This comparative study of the River Idle bridge in midsummer conditions, features perhaps the most famous Gresley pacific, A4 60022 *Mallard*, heading the down 'Flying Scotsman' in July 1960. One of four A4s built in 1938 with the Kylchap double exhaust from new (60005/22/33/34), *Mallard* achieved world renown on 6th July 1938 by descending Stoke Bank with a brake test special at a new world record speed at Milepost 91. At the time, the LNER claimed 125 mph but closer examination of the Dynamometer Car records revealed a momentary peak of 126 mph and this is the figure which is indicated on the commemorative plaque, fitted to the engine after the war to record the event. Happily *Mallard* has been restored to working order and is preserved at the NRM in full garter blue livery as LNER 4468.

At Milepost 138

BELOW: Another A4, 60029 *Woodcock* heads south away from Retford at Milepost 138, with the morning semi-fast from Leeds to King's Cross in November 1961. Built in July 1937 at Doncaster (Works No 1858), *Woodcock* was one of several A4s to come into service when new painted in LNER standard green. It later became garter blue, of course, like the rest of the class. The engine was rebuilt in October 1958 with a double Kylchap exhaust and was withdrawn in October 1963.

ABOVE: Gresley Class A3 60110 *Robert the Devil*, a Kylchap double chimney engine fitted with German trough type deflectors, heads the up 'Yorkshire Pullman' past Ordsall in November 1962. Although normally a Copley Hill A1 pacific working, the rostered engine had failed and the King's Cross A3 was substituted at short notice, making a rare sight which was much appreciated by the photographer. Built in July 1923 as an A1 pacific at Doncaster (Works No 1571), it was rebuilt in August 1942 to Class A3, fitted with a Kylchap exhaust in May 1959 and given trough deflectors in July 1961. No 60110 was withdrawn in May 1963 with a recorded mileage of 2,148,830, a good figure but well short of the highest mileage in working traffic for the class. This was achieved by sister engine 60106 *Flying Fox* with 2,642,860 miles.

BELOW: Class A3 60063 *Isinglass* heads south past Ordsall with the morning semi-fast from Leeds to King's Cross on a misty morning in November 1960. Always worked by a Top Shed (King's Cross) locomotive, this train was the return working for the engine of the previous evening's down 'Yorkshire Pullman'. In consequence, the condition of the engine was always first class and a tribute to Peter Townend and his staff at 34A. No 60063 was built in July 1925 at Doncaster (Works No 1618) as an A1 pacific, rebuilt in April 1946 as an A3 and fitted with a Kylchap double exhaust in February 1959. German trough deflectors were subsequently applied in August 1961 and the engine was withdrawn in June 1964.

ABOVE: Class B1 4-6-0 61073 passes Ordsall with an up short freight in February 1959. The rear signals indicate the train is to go into the up loop at Grove Road. Built in September 1946 by the North British Loco Co (Works No 25829), 61073 was a New England engine for most of its existence, withdrawal occurred in September 1963.

Great North Road over Great Northern Railway

BELOW: *Royal Lancer* 60107 heads a southbound express in the cutting south of the old A1 roadbridge in June 1963. Another 1923 built engine, 60107 was constructed in May at Doncaster (Works No 1568) as an A1 pacific. These were the first Gresley pacifics to be seen in quantity, just after the 1923 grouping. Mostly named after famous racehorses, they soon became famous for their exploits. In time, the A1 design evolved into the later A3 type (the original A2s were the former North Eastern pacifics) with higher boiler pressure and other improvements. These were so successful that the older A1s were gradually rebuilt as A3s, *Royal Lancer* being thus treated in October 1946. It was fitted with a Kylchap double exhaust in May 1959. German trough deflectors were added in November 1961 and the engine was withdrawn in October 1963 with a recorded mileage of 2,251,501.

ABOVE: Class V2 60906 of Doncaster shed heads south at the same location with an up special from Wakefield to King's Cross on Rugby League Cup Final day in May 1960. Working one of a dozen or more specials early that morning, 60906 was clean and working well. Built at Darlington in April 1940, 60906 is shown as built. It was subsequently rebuilt in December 1960 with separate cylinders with outside steampipes and withdrawn in May 1963.

On Gamston Curve

ABOVE: Gresley Class K3 2-6-0 61829 with a southbound mixed freight has just passed Grove Road box and level crossing on a lovely early morning in July 1959. The start of the up loop at the bottom of Gamston curve will be noted; this has now been shortened to start by Eaton Wood. Despite present day colour light signalling and lifting barriers, Grove Road box survives to this day controlling the busy road from Ordsall to Grove and Headon villages. The K3 type was the first Gresley design to incorporate the well known 2:1 conjugated lever which allowed two sets of valve gear to feed steam to three cylinders. The first examples dated from 1920 (GNR Class H4) and as LNER K3, the type was constructed until 1937. An early member of this outstandingly successful class, 61829 was built in December 1924 at Darlington and was withdrawn in February 1962.

BELOW: *Sir Nigel Gresley* heads south round Gamston curve with an up express on a lovely summer's day in August 1962. Another famous A4, 60007 was one of several 'ton up' Gresley engines, its achievement being to descend Stoke Bank, driven by Bill Hoole to a (curtailed!) maximum of 112 mph, in May 1959 with the SLS Golden Jubilee special. This turned out, in the event, to be the highest post-war steam speed record in Britain. Built in November 1937 as LNER 4498 and named after the designer in recognition of it being his 100th pacific, 60007 was fitted with a Kylchap double exhaust in December 1957. The engine was in Bill Hoole's regular charge at King's Cross and remained there until dieselisation of the GN main line in June 1963. *Sir Nigel* was then transferred to Scotland, working on the Aberdeen-Glasgow expresses until withdrawn in February 1966. Now preserved in working order as LNER 4498, *Sir Nigel Gresley* is another fine tribute to the most famous locomotive engineer of the LNER.

BELOW: Class A1 60140 *Balmoral* leans to Gamston curve with an early morning express from York to King's Cross in June 1960. Built at Darlington in December 1948 (Works No 2059) to the design of A H Peppercorn, 60140 was a York engine for most of its existence. The main A1 series was developed by Peppercorn from Thompson's unpopular 1945 rebuild of the pioneer Gresley pacific 60113 *Great Northern*. Fortunately the Peppercorn engines were as popular as 60113 was not and were amongst Britain's most reliable and trouble-free express steam types. The class mostly came into service without names but this was soon thought inappropriate for such a fine design and 60140 was named in July 1950. It lingered on at York after dieselisation of main line passenger expresses until withdrawn in January 1965, latterly working relief trains and freight on the lines north of York.

Approaching Eaton Wood

BELOW: Approaching Eaton Wood, A3 60039 *Sandwich* attacks Gamston bank in fine style with an up afternoon express in August 1961. The GNR crossing keeper's house near the rear of the train has long since vanished. Latterly a King's Cross engine, *Sandwich* was one of many which were built as the A3 type from new. It came out from Doncaster in September 1934 (Works No 1794), a Kylchap double exhaust was fitted in July 1959 and trough deflectors in June 1961. Withdrawal came in March 1963 with a recorded mileage of 1,569,085.

ABOVE: A 'Green Arrow' of Doncaster shed (60889) climbs Gamston bank near Eaton Wood with an up fitted cement train on a June morning in 1960. The nickname 'Green Arrow' was applied to the V2 class because the first example was thus named, the name itself referring to a fast overnight freight service from King's Cross Goods. Most of the rest were un-named, like the example seen here, seen in as built condition (new from Darlington in December 1939). It was subsequently rebuilt with separate cylinder castings and outside steam pipes in March 1961 and ran thus until withdrawal in June 1963. Round this area, wheat was the staple crop and many fires from stray sparks occurred, particularly in dry summers, eg 1959. nb Rebuilds of V2 had outside steam pipes and individual cylinder castings rather than the monobloc type.

BELOW: Gresley K3 61899 of Hull Dairycoates shed heads south near Eaton Wood with a long train of fish vans in August 1961. The K3 locomotives nearly always put up a good exhaust when working hard and 61899 was no exception. Built as LNER 1100 by Armstrong Whitworth (Works No 1111) in March 1931, the locomotive was the first of 40 K3s built by that company. The engine lasted until December 1962 when the surviving 20 engines were withdrawn 'en masse' and the class became extinct in operating department stock. Three K3s survived after that date as stationary boilers at New England, King's Cross and Colwick sheds, the final survivor was 61943 at Colwick, condemned in October 1965.

ABOVE: Former Great Central type 2-8-0, Class 04/3 63737 puts up a smoky exhaust climbing the long up loop near Eaton Wood with a local freight to Tuxford in August 1961. A classic Robinson GCR design, 63737 was built for the Railway Operating Division of the Royal Engineers (ROD No 1807) by North British Locomotive Co, Queen's Park Works, Glasgow, in September 1917 (Works No 21774), for wartime military service in France. It was later loaned to the London and North Western Railway becoming LNWR No 2922 from 1919 to 1921, after which it was returned to ROD store at Queensferry. It was subsequently purchased by the LNER and taken into traffic in September 1927 as LNER No 6564. Withdrawal occurred in December 1962.

Eaton Wood Road Bridge

BELOW: The solitary Class A1/1, 60113 *Great Northern*, already described earlier, is seen here climbing Gamston bank with an up express in August 1962. Taken from the nearby road, this is a favourite picture with a tree frame. Although nominally a Thompson rebuild of Gresley A1 4470 *Great Northern* in September 1945, very little of the original engine was used; the tender itself was built in 1937, the original coal-railed tender being then transferred to another pacific. An A4 type boiler (Diagram 107) was used in the new engine and originally, straight nameplates were carried on the smokebox sides. Large straight-sided smoke deflectors were fitted in December 1945 and the nameplates transferred to these. New plates with smaller Gill Sans lettering with the GNR coat of arms replaced the earlier plates in May 1951.

The use of the Class designation A1 for the new post-war large-wheeled pacifics (including 60113) caused the remaining Gresley A1s (ie those which had not yet been rebuilt to A3) to be reclassified A10 until such time as all had been converted to A3. *Great Northern* itself was withdrawn in November 1962.

ABOVE: In this view, K3 61981 heads an up late afternoon excursion just south of Eaton Wood road bridge in October 1961. Though built as mixed traffic engines, K3s were mostly used on fast freight duties for which their 5ft 8in wheels were ideal. But, like many other 2-6-0s from all four British companies, the leading pair of carrying wheels gave considerable stability which, combined with adequate boiler and tractive power, made them ideally suited for passenger working of this kind where really high speed would be unlikely. Built at Darlington in December 1936 (Works number not issued) as LNER 3821, 61981 was withdrawn in November 1962. The engine is putting up a fine exhaust climbing the 3½ miles of 1:178/200 gradient of Gamston bank to the summit at Markham Moor.

Eaton Wood Road – Gamston

BELOW: Another picture at the Eaton Wood road bridge shows Gresley Class 02/2 63933 climbing Gamston bank with a heavy southbound morning freight in July 1961. Two ex-GNR tenders converted as sludge carriers for the Muskham water troughs plant near the River Trent can be seen next to the engine.

The 02 Class was developed from Gresley's (and Britain's) first 3-cylinder engine to use only two sets of valve gear (GNR 461 of 1918). The main series was built from 1921 onwards using the 2:1 lever arrangement introduced with the K3s a year earlier. Though never as numerous as the K3s, the O2s were a fine design and many were built by the LNER, later examples from 1932 onwards having side-window cabs. No 63933 was built at Doncaster works in October 1923 (Works No 1575), the GN type cab (as built) was replaced with the later style of side-window cab in January 1958. The engine was withdrawn in December 1962.

ABOVE: In this view, V2 60848 heads an up express between Eaton Wood bridge and Gamston box in August 1961.

This type of working was somewhat less common at this time but was very characteristic of this class during the war and in the early 1950s. The V2s had 6ft 2in driving wheels (a dimension bequeathed to the later Class A2 pacifics) and their tractive power was equal to that of an A3 — facts of which both the LNER and BR took full advantage. Originally a Scottish area engine based at St Margarets and Haymarket sheds from new, 60848 was subsequently transferred to Doncaster. Built as LNER 4819 at Darlington in March 1939, the engine survived with monobloc cylinders and single chimney until withdrawn in July 1962.

Around Gamston Box

BELOW: Class B1 4-6-0 61282 heads an up parcels train near Gamston signal box on a lovely June afternoon in 1960. The up loop from Grove Road box ended here and a truncated version is retained today, but the small isolated signal box has long since vanished. No 61282 was built by the North British Loco Co in January 1948 (Works No 26183) and was withdrawn in September 1962. Originally a Great Eastern section locomotive, allocated to Stratford shed, it was transferred to the GN section on dieselisation of its former GE territory.

The Class B1 was probably Edward Thompson's most successful design and 410 were eventually built, some with names. Though not, perhaps, as well-known as the more numerous LMS Stanier Class 5, Thompson's design was very much influenced by the LMS product and was intended for similar duties.

BELOW: Class A3 60078 *Night Hawk* heads the newly introduced 'Anglo-Scottish Car Carrier' train near Gamston box in June 1960. The headboard is of note being of the pre-war type with white background and black lettering.

This type of working was one of the more successful attempts by the railway to meet the growing motor car competition and, of course, 'Motorail' services are still a common feature of operation both in Britain and overseas.

Night Hawk was based at Gateshead and was exceptionally clean for an engine from this depot. No 60078 was built as an A1 Pacific, LNER 2577, by the North British Loco Co in October 1924 (Works No 23115); it was rebuilt to Class A3 in January 1944 and a Kylchap double chimney was fitted in February 1959. Trough deflectors were added in March 1962 and the engine was withdrawn seven months later with a recorded mileage of 2,229,140.

ABOVE: One-time ROD 2-8-0, now Class 04/8 No 63647, heads an up freight of flat bogies round the start of the long curve from Gamston box to Askham tunnel in May 1960. The isolated Gamston box is seen on the left hand side of the train. No 63647 was built in February 1918 by Kitson & Co (Works No 5788) for the ROD (No 1606) and saw service in France. The engine was repatriated and stored at Morecambe after cessation of hostilities. The engine was loaned to the Great Central Railway from 1919 to 1921 and then replaced in store. The LNER purchased it in February 1927 and it became 6544 entering traffic in December 1928 as Class 04/2. This style of rebuild was introduced in 1944 by Thompson, using a B1 type boiler and a new side-window cab; but the GC origins still remained fairly obvious. The engine was rebuilt to Class 04/8 in March 1958 and withdrawn in May 1964.

Approaching Askham Tunnel

BELOW: Class A3 60054 *Prince of Wales* heads an up express nearing Askham tunnel in August 1961. Built as an A1 pacific at Doncaster Works in December 1924 (Works No 1609) as LNER 2553, *Manna*, it was renamed in December 1926 and rebuilt to Class A3 in July 1943. The name *Manna* re-appeared later on another engine which became 60085 in BR days. The coal-railed tender reveals its early origin. This tender style was very much a GNR design and it was some time before the more familiar high sided LNER tenders began to become the standard for new 4-6-2 construction. Many A3s retained the older sort of tender to the very end, despite many changes to the locomotive itself. A double chimney was fitted in August 1958, trough deflectors were added in May 1962 and the engine withdrawn in June 1964 having run 1,862,818 miles.

A4s at Markham Moor

ABOVE: *Silver Link* again — here seen climbing from the short Askham tunnel to Markham Moor summit with the up 'Elizabethan' in August 1961. 60014 was a regular performer on this long distance non-stop Edinburgh Waverley to King's Cross express and completed the 392.7 mile run in a schedule of 6½ hours.

For the non-stop workings, the Gresley pacifics received special corridor tenders to allow crews to change over at the half-way point (generally just north of York). The relief crew travelled in the train until this point. The earliest corridor tenders were built in 1928 to allow the original Gresley pacifics to work non-stop, but by BR days, the A4s were the only engines to be so equipped. Even so, there were never as many corridor tenders as A4s (23 out of 34 in early BR days) so not all the A4s were able to work this famous train. The non-stop distinction was first applied to the 'Flying Scotsman' train but after the war, it was transferred to the 'Capitals Limited' (renamed 'Elizabethan' in 1953).

BELOW: Class A4 No 60008 *Dwight D Eisenhower* heads a down King's Cross to Newcastle express at Markham Moor summit in March 1960, about to begin the 3½ mile descent to Retford. Note the horsebox next to the tender, a quite common feature of express trains in steam days. No 60008 was built as LNER 4496 *Golden Shuttle* in September 1937 at Doncaster (Works No 1861). This was one of two special names (the other being *Golden Fleece*) which were given to the engines allocated to the 'West Riding Limited' streamlined train, a contemporary of the more famous 'Coronation' and formed from identical special stock. *Golden Fleece* was not renamed and became BR 60030.

Golden Shuttle was renamed in September 1945 in honour of the famous American general and was fitted with a Kylchap double chimney in August 1958. It was withdrawn in July 1963 and restored to final condition and livery at Doncaster Works, prior to its presentation on the 27th April 1964 by Dr R Beeching to the National Railway Museum of Green Bay, Wisconsin, USA, where it has been on exhibition ever since. This locomotive (like *Mallard* in its record-breaking form) was one of several A4s *not* to carry a corridor tender.

Northbound Expresses

BELOW: Class A3 No 60059 *Tracery* heads a down express at Markham Moor summit in June 1962 before descending to Retford. *Tracery* was built at Doncaster in March 1925 (Works No 1614) as an A1 pacific and was rebuilt as an A3 in July 1942. Fitted with a Kylchap double chimney in July 1958 and trough deflectors in September 1961, it was finally withdrawn in December 1962 with a noteworthy recorded mileage of 2,523,843.

OPPOSITE: Class V2 60849 puts up a fine show for the camera, having come over the summit at Markham Moor in June 1960 with a down express. No 60849 was built at Darlington Works in March 1939 and lasted until April 1962 with its original monobloc cylinders and single chimney.

East Coast Pullmans

TOP: Pullman trains on the East Coast Main Line always formed a colourful attraction and four photographs are included in the next pages. Here, Class A4 60029 *Woodcock* comes over Markham Moor summit with the down 'Harrogate Sunday Pullman' in November 1961. This was the Sunday equivalent of the 'Yorkshire Pullman' but ran much earlier in the day and was headed by A4, A3 and A1 Class pacifics indiscriminately; the A1s usually had the weekday train. The engines worked as far as Leeds Central, where the train reversed for the final 'leg' to Harrogate. No 60029 was built at Doncaster Works in July 1937 (Works No 1858) as LNER 4493 in apple green livery, it was rebuilt with a double chimney in October 1958 and withdrawn in October 1963.

BOTTOM: The up 'Tees-Tyne Pullman' on Christmas Eve 1959 runs past Ordsall headed by Class A4 60022 *Mallard*. This was normally an English Electric Type 4 diesel diagram by then, but as seemed usual, the A4 class dominated the working due to diesel non-availability. At this time, *Mallard* was one of the many A4s with a corridor tender but when restored for preservation, it was given back the non-corridor type appropriate to its record-breaking condition.

It is worth noting that 1959-60 was to see the last regular workings of full-sets of 'slab-sided' Pullmans on the East Coast route. In 1960, many of them began to be replaced by the new Metro-Cammell cars with BR Mk 1 curved-side body shells.

BELOW: Another photograph of the down 'Harrogate Sunday Pullman' in November 1961 shows the train this time headed by clean Class A1 60120 *Kittiwake*. The engine is recovering from a signal check just south of Retford crossing and makes a fine picture in the misty sunshine. Note how the mixture of newer and older Pullman cars makes the train itself seem more 'untidy' than in the slab-sided period. No 60120 was built at Doncaster in December 1948 (Works No 2037), was named in May 1950 and ran until January 1964, working from Copley Hill depot for most of its 15 year life span.

Dignity and Impudence

ABOVE: This picture shows a further Pullman working that should not have been steam-hauled:— Class A2/2 No 60502 *Earl Marischal* heading the down 'Queen of Scots' Pullmans nearing Retford one Saturday in August 1960. This engine was the Peterborough replacement for a Type 4 English Electric diesel which had failed and it produced a rare colour photograph.

Earl Marischal in the form shown here was one of several of Edward Thompson's less than happy experiments with former Gresley designs. In this case he took Gresley's Class P2 2-8-2s (the famous 'Cock o' the North' design) and turned them into 4-6-2s, officially to reduce the rigid wheelbase and make them less critical on the constantly curving tracks north of Edinburgh. They were never well-liked as 4-6-2s, though still very powerful with their original 6ft 2in wheels. No 60502 was rebuilt from Gresley P2 2-8-2 2002 in June 1944 at Doncaster (Works No 1796). The engine was the last A2/2 Pacific in working stock being withdrawn in July 1961.

BELOW: This interesting photograph shows a regular Saturday working involving a Retford Class B1 locomotive. No 61231 passes the GC loco shed at Thrumpton with the front footplate loaded with churns filled with drinking water for the isolated road crossings and signal boxes on the GC lines to Gainsborough and the GN main line both south and north of Retford. Being without piped water, this was the only way of delivery for them. The engine was built in September 1947 by the North British Loco Co (Works No 26132); withdrawal occurred in July 1962.

Trial Trips – Ex-Works

ABOVE: Class A4 60034 *Lord Faringdon*, ex-works and fully repainted is seen running through Retford station returning from Barkston to Doncaster late on a June 1962 afternoon. This was its last heavy overhaul and repaint at Doncaster. Originally named *Peregrine*, 60034 was built in July 1938 as LNER 4903 and was the final engine of the 35 strong A4 class, a total reduced to 34 by a German bomb at York during the war. The engine was fitted with a Kylchap double chimney from new and was a GN section engine until sent to Scotland in the latter part of 1963. Stationed at Ferryhill shed, Aberdeen, for use on the three-hour expresses to Glasgow, 60034 was withdrawn in August 1966, being the penultimate engine at work — save, of course for those preserved.

BELOW: In this picture, K3 61934, a fully repainted Tweedmouth engine makes slow progress up the main line near Askham tunnel on the way to Barkston in June 1960. Built by R Stephenson & Co in December 1934 as LNER 1307, it was always a North Eastern area engine and was withdrawn in November 1962.

GN Freight Locos

ABOVE: 02/2 2-8-0 Class 63936 stands in Retford GC shed yard in June 1962 and shows evidence of recent cleaning. Built at Doncaster as LNER 3491 in December 1923 (Works No 1578) with a GN style cab but to LNER loading gauge, 63936 was withdrawn in September 1963.

BELOW: Retford (GC) shed also housed ex-GNR Class J6 0-6-0 locomotives, and 64178, in very clean condition, is seen waiting for the road to Worksop near the GC/GN crossing in October 1958. An ex-LMS brake van forms the load and a veteran driver watches the photographer. The J6 design was one of two types of superheated 0-6-0 introduced during Gresley's first two years as CME of the old Great Northern, but was in most essentials, virtually an Ivatt design. The example illustrated was built in November 1911 at Doncaster (Works No 1319), and was withdrawn in April 1960.

Retford Thrumpton GC Shed

ABOVE: One of the final series of O2 2-8-0s built in December 1942 as LNER 3850 (Doncaster Works No 1948), Class O2/3 63980 takes water at Retford GC shed in April 1963. The pristine condition of this heavy freight engine at such a late date for Eastern Region steam is worthy of note.

BELOW: A general view of Retford (GC) shed in April 1963 with two Class O2 2-8-0s and a Class O4 2-8-0 in view. Although having but three shed roads, a substantial yard was situated at the east end of the shed. Retford GC achieved fame with its stud of both ex-GCR and ex-GNR design freight engines, most of which were kept in clean condition.

GC Line Freights

BELOW: Class J11 0-6-0 64451 nears the Retford GC/GN crossing with an eastbound freight in April 1959. The J11 type dated back to 1901 and was a typically robust Robinson design for the old Great Central. Built with slide valves and non-superheated, the engines had a long and very useful life. Many detail variations existed (boiler mountings, tender types etc.) but the only significant mechanical variations were on the J11/3 rebuilds (1942 and later) with long travel piston valves and higher boiler pitch. The example here, however, is one of the original slide valve engines (which represented by far the bigger part of the total class), built at Gorton works in April 1910 and withdrawn in December 1959.

ABOVE: Class WD 2-8-0 90662 moves a heavy train of miscellaneous empty coke wagons over the Retford GC/GN crossing and heads towards Whisker Hill Junction and Worksop in October 1963. The rear of the crossing box can be seen.

The Class WD (War Department) was very much a 'utility' design dating from 1943 when R A Riddles conceived it as a 'cheap and cheerful' alternative to the more expensive-to-produce Stanier LMS Class 8F 2-8-0, the first British 2-8-0 type to be bought by the WD for overseas use during the 1939-45 war. Appearances notwithstanding, they were derived in part from the LMS design and 90662 was built by the Vulcan Foundry in September 1944 (Works No 5127) as WD 79184. It was loaned to the LNER from August 1947 until purchase by British Railways in 1948. No 90662 was withdrawn in August 1965, being cut up at Draper's yard in Hull in January 1966.

GC Passenger at Whisker Hill

BELOW: Former GC 'Director' Class D11 4-4-0 62668 *Jutland* puts up a heavy exhaust climbing to Whisker Hill Junction with a Lincoln to Sheffield train on a Sunday morning in May 1959. Obviously, being just ex-winter storage at Darnall shed, 62668 was a little rusty. The Lincoln train had taken the normal route into Retford station but failed to start the heavy train on the sharp Sheffield line curve and had to reverse out onto the GC line for a good start on the direct freight line to Whisker Hill and the three mile climb to Checker House.

The Robinson 'Directors' were an outstanding example of the British 'inside-cylinder' 4-4-0 type and were introduced in 1920, *Jutland* being built in November 1922 just prior to the formation of the LNER. Gresley was sufficiently impressed to order more of them for the LNER in 1924, with few significant modifications, and they lasted well. The pioneer engine (GCR 506 *Butler Henderson* and sister to *Jutland*) is preserved, but 62668 was withdrawn for scrap in November 1960.

ABOVE: B1 61212 of Retford shed passes Whisker Hill Junction box off the curves from Retford station with the every other Saturday football supporters excursion from Retford to Wadsley Bridge, (Hillsborough) for Sheffield Wednesday's ground in September 1962. The train called at all stations en-route. The train is mostly composed of BR standard stock but a former Gresley LNER brake third in surprisingly smart condition for the time is seen as the leading coach. 61212 was built in July 1947 by North British Loco Co (Queens Park Works), Works No 26113 and was withdrawn in November 1964.

Consolidated Freight

ABOVE: Class O4/8 2-8-0 63788 approaches Thrumpton crossing with an eastbound coke train in April 1963. Retford crossing box and station can be seen in the background and Thrumpton GC box is on the left. No 63788 was built in June 1918 as ROD 1886 by the North British Loco Co (Hyde Park Works), Works No 21863, for service in France. After the end of the war, it was loaned to the GCR from 1919 to 1921 then stored at Morecambe before purchase by the LNER in 1927 becoming No 6592. It was rebuilt to Class O4/5 in September 1939; rebuilt again, more comprehensively, to Class O4/8 in March 1957 and was withdrawn in March 1966.

BELOW: Gresley Class O2/3 63986 approaches Retford station on the GN main line passing North box with an Aldwarke to High Dyke iron ore empties train. These workings to and from High Dyke (a junction just to the Grantham side of Stoke Tunnel) were a characteristic feature of East Coast operations for many a long year and their passing when the ironstone quarries closed was sadly missed by many enthusiasts. This classic Retford location was used by many photographers going back to pre-war days. No 63986 was the penultimate member of the Class O2 series being built at Doncaster Works in January 1943 (Works No 1954). It was withdrawn in June 1963, having enjoyed only about half the lifetime of the older members of the series.

LM Visitors

ABOVE: Former LMS Class 8P 4-6-2 46245 *City of London* shows the maroon BR livery to good effect climbing Gamston bank with a return excursion from Doncaster to King's Cross in June 1963. The engine was a welcome visitor to the GN main line on a lovely June day and was one of sixteen members of Stanier's famous 'Coronation' ('Duchess') Class to be given what amounted to the old pre-war LMS Crimson Lake livery during 1957-64.

BELOW: LMS design locomotives in the shape of Stanier Class 8F 2-8-0s were almost daily visitors to Retford on the Nottingham to Doncaster and return freight working from Newark where they joined the GN main line. In June 1960, 48360 attacks Gamston bank with the southbound freight; it was a Northampton (2E) engine whose depot supplied the power for this working.

Some Class 8Fs were also built for the LNER during the war years and others by the LNER for the LMS. This was because after the WD type had been adopted for military use overseas, the wartime Railway Executive committee decided that the LMS design should be standardised for 'home' consumption and examples were, in fact, constructed by all four main line companies. Their presence on ex-LNER lines was not, therefore, unusual, though 48360 was a genuine ex-LMS machine (built at Horwich in 1944).

North of Retford

ABOVE: Class A1 60145 *St Mungo* leaves Retford with a King's Cross to Leeds express in March 1963 just north of Babworth bridge. The GN main line to the north of Retford was relatively level and not as attractive for photography as the southern end of Retford. By the time this view was taken, many workings had been handed over to diesels. But the A1s were relatively new machines and had an excellent reputation for high mileages, both annually and between heavy overhauls. During the early 1950s, they bore the main burden of heavy East Coast express workings until the Gresley pacifics were given a renewed lease of life and it is sad that none are preserved. However, they lasted longer than many during the 1960s and 60145 (built at Darlington Works in March 1949 —Works No 2064) was withdrawn in June 1966 as the last of the class. It was named in August 1950.

GN/GC Crossing

BELOW: One of the main features which often differentiates the modern railway from its steam-hauled predecessor is the massive reduction in freight traffic. So it is perhaps fitting that this survey should conclude with a typical yet now long-vanished East-Coast style goods train of the steam age:— Class O2/4 63949 heading an eastbound freight around the Lincoln line curve from the GN to the GC line at Retford station in May 1960. The main line crossing and signal box form part of the picture with numerous signal wires, point rodding and telegraph wires — the ground wires and rodding made lineside walking very hazardous in this area.